James Dean

A LIFE IN PICTURES

James Dean

A LIFE IN PICTURES

Marie Clayton

BARNES & NOBLE

NEW YORK

ISBN-13: 978-0-7607-5614-0
ISBN-10: 0-7607-5614-7

Produced by Atlantic Publishing

Printed and bound in China by SNP Leefung Printers Limited

3   5   7   9   10   8   6   4

Photo Credits

Bettman/Corbis:
10, 11, 12, 14, 15, 16 top, 16 bottom, 17 top, 18 top, 18 bottom, 35, 36,
37, 40, 44, 48, 61, 63, 64, 65 top, 65 bottom, 84 bottom, 85, 87 top, 87 bottom,
88, 89 top, 90 top, 90 bottom, 91

Warner Bros., courtesy of The Aquarius Collection:
2, 6, 8, 9, 13, 17 bottom, 19, 20 top, 20 bottom, 21, 22 top,
24, 25, 26, 27 top, 27 bottom, 28, 29 top, 29 bottom, 30 top, 30 bottom, 31 top, 31 bottom,
32 top, 32 bottom, 33, 34, 38, 39, 41 top, 41 bottom, 42, 43, 45, 46, 47, 49 top, 49 bottom, 50, 51, 52,
53 top, 53 bottom, 54, 55 top, 55 bottom, 56 top, 56 bottom, 57, 58, 59 top, 59 bottom, 60 top,
60 bottom, 62 top, 62 bottom, 66, 67, 68, 69 top, 69 bottom, 70, 71 top, 71 bottom, 72 top, 72 bottom,
73, 74 top, 74 bottom, 75, 76, 77, 78 top, 78 bottom, 79, 81, 82, 84 top, 86, 89 bottom, 92, 93
The Aquarius Collection:
22 bottom, 23, 80, 83

Dedication

For William and Emily Clayton

CONTENTS

Introduction
8

Chapter One
The Early Years
12

Chapter Two
East of Eden
24

Chapter Three
Rebel Without a Cause
38

Chapter Four
Giant
66

Chapter Five
Genius Never Dies
80

Epilogue
92

Chronology and Filmography
94

Index
96

Introduction

Opposite: A still from *Giant*, Jimmy's last movie. Although he did not agree with how the director saw the role, Jimmy still gave a remarkable performance as Jett Rink, and when the film was released a year after his death he was nominated for an Oscar.

Above: Jimmy with Natalie Wood in a scene from *Rebel Without a Cause*. While Jimmy's relationships with his male co-stars were sometimes strained, actresses who worked closely with him responded well and were very often protective of him.

Right: After years of performing on the stage, on television shows, and in films, Jimmy was supremely confident in front of the camera. He was aware of the importance of building an image, and once asked a photographer not to publish a picture because it made him look too vulnerable.

Opposite: Cal and Abra embrace in a still from *East of Eden.*

In his short career James Dean starred in only three major pictures, but each is now regarded as a classic of the cinema. Two of the films were released after his death, so the excitement at his screen presence and original characterization was tinged with deep sorrow at the tragic loss of such a stupendous talent before it had time to develop fully. In his movies James Dean played a young rebel, challenging authority and questioning accepted ways of behavior—but also an outsider with a troubled home life looking for love. To some extent this mirrored his own life—his mother died when he was still just a child, and although he was loved by the aunt and uncle who brought him up, he felt rejected by his father.

At an early age Jimmy developed an interest in acting, and his unusual talent was very quickly apparent. Despite this, his assurance and his determination to do things his way alienated some of those who could have helped him, while his good looks and muscular physique attracted both women and men who

were more interested in his physical attributes than his acting talents. However, he eventually got the break he was hoping for when he was offered a major part in *The Immoralist* as the blackmailing Arab servant who seduces his male employer. When the play opened on Broadway Jimmy's performance was stunning, and he was soon offered his first movie role, in *East of Eden*. His universal attraction translated onto the screen—girls fell in love with him and boys wanted to be him.

Jimmy believed totally in Method acting but pushed the concept to its limits, striving to show how a real person would behave and daring to go where others would not. Actors who were classically trained, who knew their lines and hit their marks, did not understand Jimmy's apparently chaotic approach, but in the end even they had to admit that the result was an extraordinary performance that was often unnerving in its accuracy. His influence on modern acting styles has been immense, despite his small body of work.

Jimmy appeared on the scene in the mid-1950s, when those

in charge were determined to maintain the status quo and uphold the American way of life. The government of the day believed that enforcing the standards of society as a whole was more important than the rights and beliefs of the individual. Those growing up under this rule soon began to see it as oppression and began to rebel openly against authority—and in Jimmy they found a hero and role model. Unlike other movie stars, he dressed casually, slouched across the screen, and looked out at the world with a mixture of resentment and contempt. He was young, bold, and determined not to submit to authority or compromise on his freedom, but he was also handsome, sensitive, and lovable. It was an irresistible combination, threatening to those in charge, but inspiring to those looking to find their way in the world. After his death he came to be widely regarded as the quintessential rebel

and became an icon to thousands of people all round the globe.

He could be wonderful company and a generous friend, but he was also a troubled young man, often given to periods of introspection and depression. He inspired strong feelings in those who met him—either they loved him or they had no time for him.

In the end, the facts cannot begin to explain the legend that has grown up around his name. He was a remarkable and original actor, who made three great movies in just over a year, but he also found a voice and a persona that spoke to an entire generation and continues to strike a chord today. Jimmy Dean the man died in a tragic accident many years ago, but James Dean is still with us—genius never dies.

Chapter One

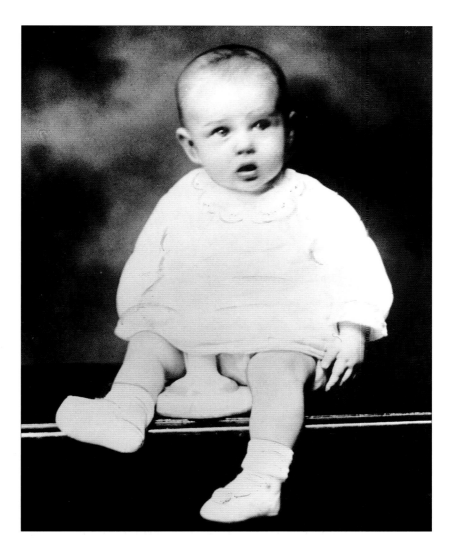

The Early Years

Above: James Byron Dean was born on February 8, 1931, in his parents' apartment. There is no record of why Winton and Mildred Dean selected the name Byron, but Winton had a friend called Byron Vice. However, Mildred loved poetry, so her baby could just as easily have been named after Lord Byron.

Opposite: Jimmy as a toddler. For the first few months of his life his parents lived in Marion, Indiana, but they later moved back to Winton's hometown of Fairmount. Fairmount was a Quaker community that had been founded by Joseph Winslow—an ancestor of Jimmy's uncle, Marcus Winslow.

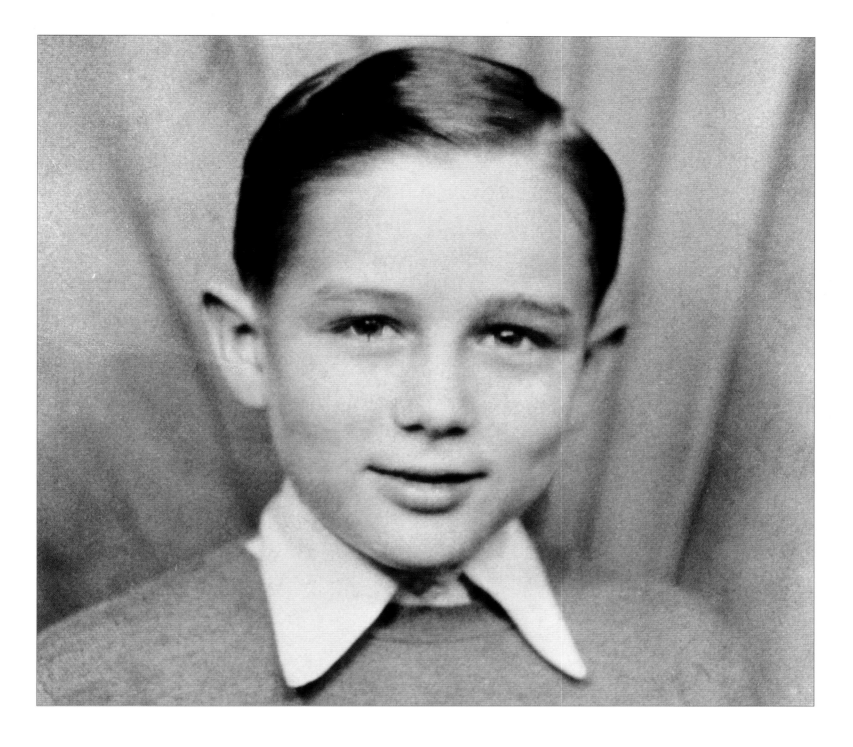

Opposite: When Jimmy was four years old his father was transferred to Sawtelle Veterans' Hospital in Santa Monica, California. The Deans moved to the West Coast, and Mildred enrolled Jimmy in violin lessons and dance classes. She had always been interested in the arts herself, and she passed on her love of performance to her son.

Above: Jimmy was only nine when his mother died of cancer, and he never got over her loss—mother and son had always been very close. Afterward, Jimmy was sent to live with his father's sister, Ortense, and her husband, Marcus, on their farm in Fairmount. Despite the circumstances of his arrival, Jimmy was not unhappy on the farm. Ortense and Marcus loved him, he had children to play with, and he settled in well at school. As he grew up, he became interested in acting, encouraged by his drama teacher.

Left: Jimmy displays an early ability to relate to the camera. As a young boy he showed an interest in acting, and often chatted to Ortense about his plans to be in the movies. She did not take him very seriously—after all, he was just an Indiana farmboy—but she underestimated his drive to perform.

Right: When Jimmy was twelve, Ortense Winslow gave birth to a son, named Marcus Junior—or Markie, as he was soon dubbed. Since Jimmy now thought of Marcus and Ortense as Mom and Dad, Jimmy was delighted to have a younger brother. Here, Jimmy and Markie play in the garden.

Left: Jimmy at home on the farm in Indiana. Jimmy enjoyed working on the land and with the animals, and in his first studio press release he would say, "Cows, pigs, chickens, and horses may not appear to be first-rate dramatic coaches, but believe it or not I learned a lot about acting from them. Working on a farm gave me an insight on life which has been of tremendous help to me in my character portrayals."

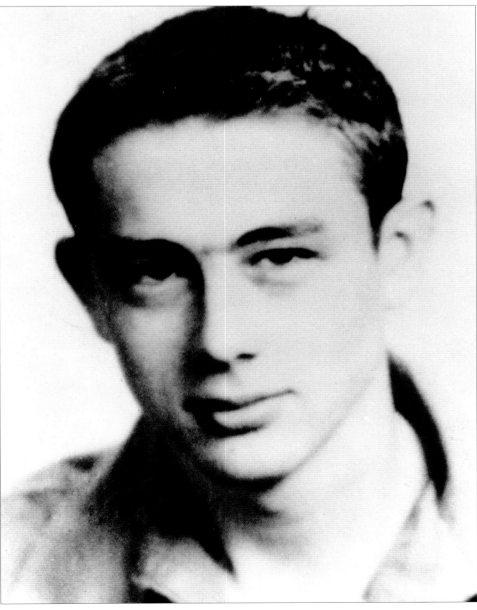

Right: Jimmy as a teenager. At about this time he became friendly with the local Wesleyan minister, the Rev. James DeWeerd, who was sophisticated and a man of the world despite his calling. He shared Jimmy's love of the arts, but also introduced him to the joys of motor racing.

Above: The Fairmount High School baseball team. Jimmy is in the center of the front row, wearing his glasses. He was extremely nearsighted, and wore special glasses that would not fall off when playing sports.

Right: The high school basketball star. Fairmount's team was known as the Quakers.

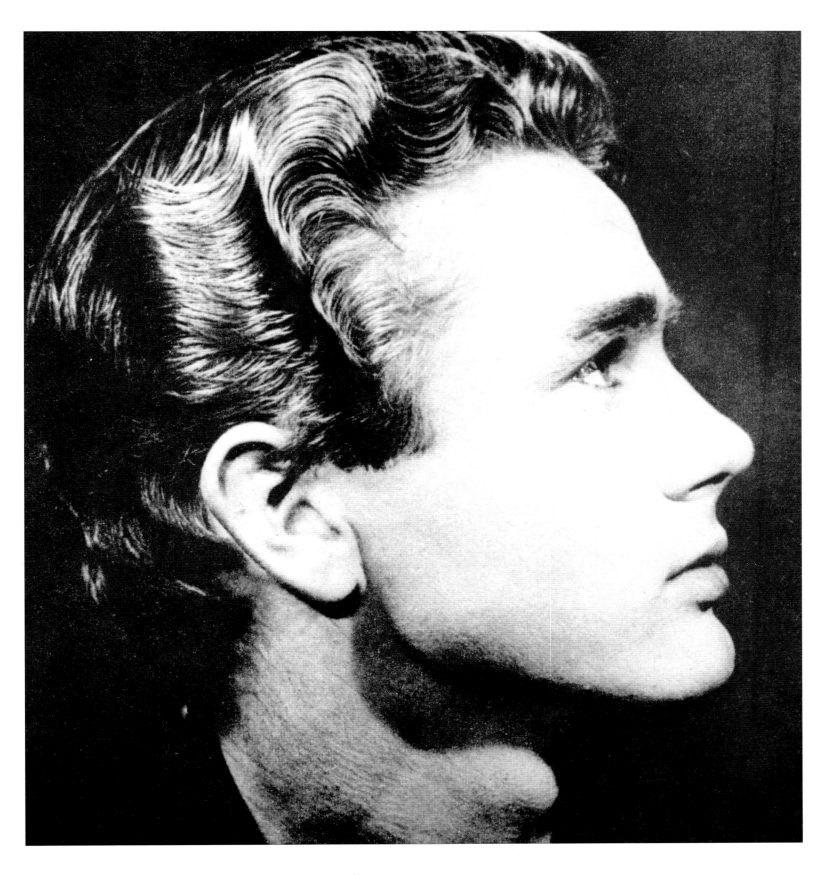

Above: One of the photographs on an early casting sheet produced for directors. Agent Isabelle Draesemer came backstage when Jimmy was appearing as Malcolm in the UCLA production of *Macbeth* and offered to represent him. Soon after, he started the round of auditions in earnest and dropped out of UCLA, although he was getting little work. Within a year, he gave up on Hollywood and went to New York to try the theater instead. In New York he became a member of the Actors Studio, where he pursued his interest in Method acting.

Above and below: After his acclaimed performance in the Broadway play *See the Jaguar* at the end of 1952, Jimmy was offered a succession of television parts, and he worked nearly continuously throughout 1953. He also did a screen test for a part in the film *Battle Cry*, but lost out to Tab Hunter.

Above: In the Broadway play *The Immoralist*, a young archaeologist takes his new wife on a honeymoon to North Africa, where he is seduced and blackmailed by their Arab houseboy. Geraldine Page played the wife, who takes to the bottle when she finds out that her husband is homosexual. Jimmy's performance as the boy, Bachir, was so riveting on opening night that audiences were stunned, but despite his triumph he resigned from the play that night because he had already been offered his first film role, in Elia Kazan's *East of Eden*.

Left: For his part as Bachir, Jimmy's light hair was dyed much darker and he wore heavy brown makeup. After he left the play he was quick to return to normal. One sequence in *The Immoralist* became legendary—the Scissors Dance. Jimmy danced seductively across the stage dressed in a loose robe, snipping lightly at the air with a pair of bright silver scissors. He explained to his friend Jonathan Gilmore that he was symbolically snipping away at the strings holding back the character played by Louis Jourdan, thus drawing him into a homosexual relationship.

Above: Jimmy performs for the still photographer. At the beginning of 1954 Dean's experience of working in Hollywood movies had been limited to bit parts in *Sailor Beware*, *Fixed Bayonets*, and *Has Anybody Seen My Gal?*, but now he was on the verge of stardom.

Opposite below: Jimmy in New York. When he first arrived in 1951 he had very little money—and what he did have he spent on seeing movies. Although he had few contacts he was always confident that he would succeed there because he believed that New Yorkers would judge him on his talent.

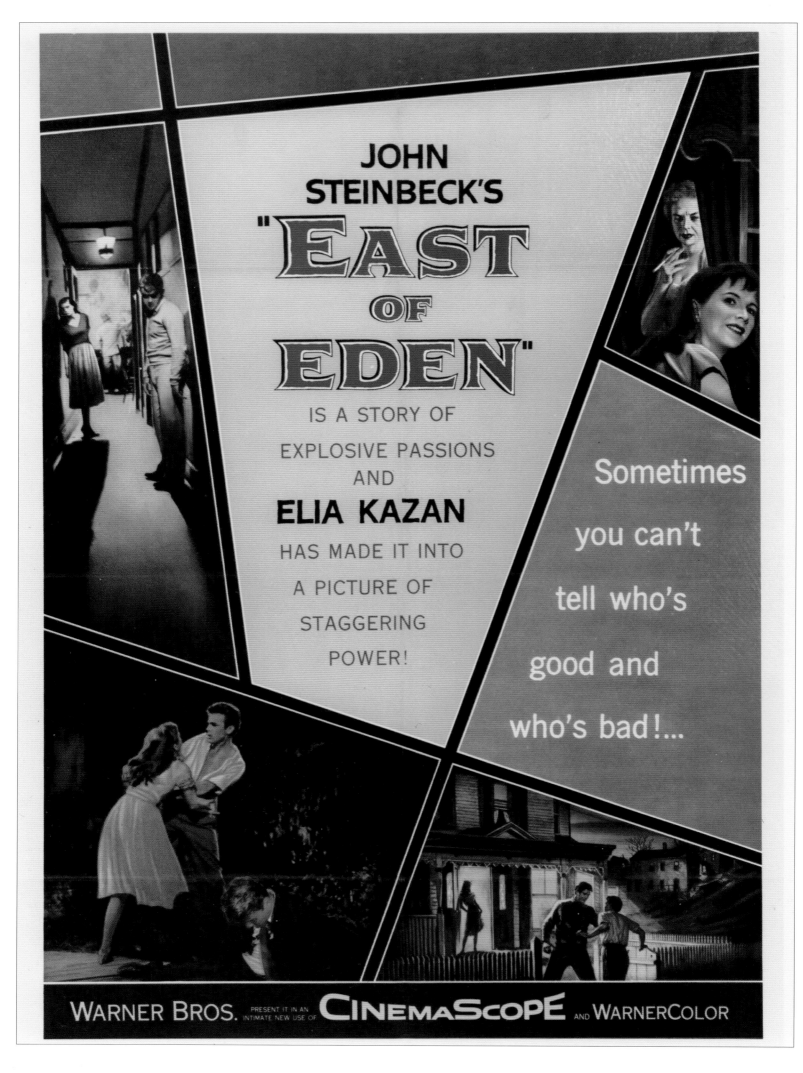

Chapter Two

East of Eden

Above: Jimmy as a despondent Cal in *East of Eden*. In many ways, the storyline picked up elements of Jimmy's own life—like Cal, he felt his father did not love him.

Opposite: As a founding member of the Actors Studio, director Elia Kazan already knew Jimmy—but it was scriptwriter Paul Osborn who suggested he would be suitable to play Cal.

Above: Steinbeck's book *East of Eden* spans fifty years and tells the story of two families, but the movie was based only on the last section. It concentrated on the Trask family and simplified the character of Cal, making him much more sympathetic. The picture opens with Jimmy as Cal loitering in the street, following a woman he thinks may be his mother.

Above: Shooting started in May 1954 in Mendocino. Although progress was slow, Jimmy and Kazan worked well together. Jimmy's approach to acting was based on instinct and emotion and he needed time to prepare himself for each scene, no matter how short. Kazan was willing to allow Jimmy to express himself and understood his reluctance to play a scene exactly according to the director's orders, which Jimmy considered to be simply following instructions, not acting.

Right: Jimmy and Timothy Carey discuss their scene on location in Mendocino.

Above: Although Jimmy was always happy to pose for the camera, he was wary of talking to the press. He told his friends that he wanted to be judged by his performance, not by how well he played the publicity game. He could be cooperative with journalists he liked, but he upset influential columnist Hedda Hopper with his surly attitude. Despite this, he almost always got good reviews—as he had hoped, in the final analysis he was judged by his talent.

Left: In this scene with Richard Davalos, which did not appear in the final cut of the film, Cal talks of how he cannot win the love of their father. Dean's moving performance powerfully conveyed Cal's sense of alienation and loss.

Below: Burl Ives and Jimmy play together on set. Studio press releases suggested that Jimmy usually preferred to spend his time alone in his dressing room listening to classical music in order to maintain the emotional intensity of his character.

Above: Although Jimmy was a genuine farmboy, Kazan sent him off to the desert before filming started to put on some weight and get a suntan for his role as Cal.

Right: Elia Kazan (left) talks to Jimmy and Lois Smith, who played the barmaid in the brothel. Despite having to work within the constraints of the 1950s Production Code, Kazan managed to evoke the louche atmosphere of a brothel.

Left: Actress Pier Angeli visits Jimmy on set. She and Jimmy were originally paired by the studio to generate publicity, but soon found a genuine liking for each other.

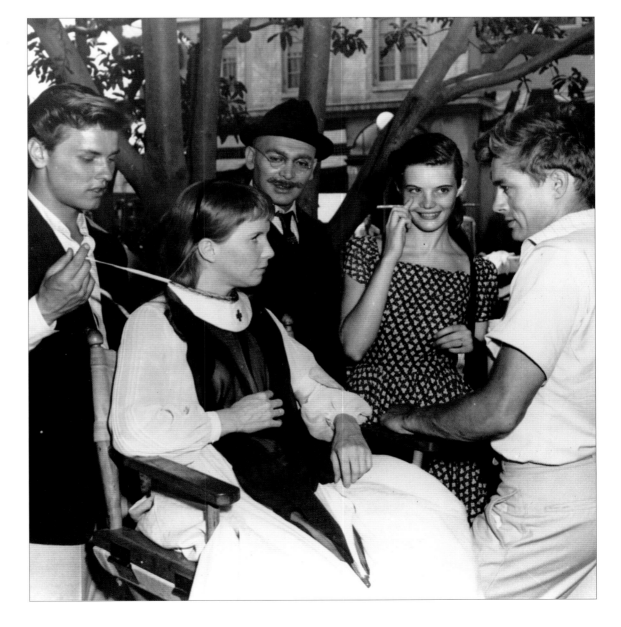

Right: Jimmy chats to some of the other actors on set. Richard Davalos played Aron, Cal's lovable brother, and Julie Harris was Abra, Aron's girlfriend. Behind them is Harold Gordon—the German shopkeeper—and Lois Smith. Although they didn't become great friends, Jimmy and Richard Davalos shared an apartment (at 3908 W. Olive) for part of the time the movie was being shot.

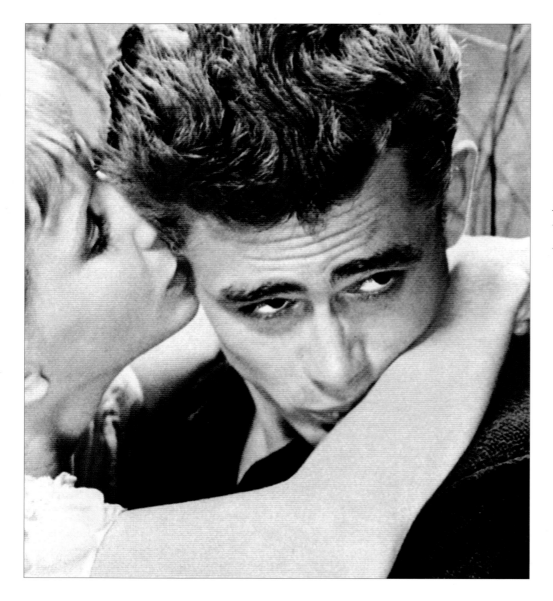

Left: Abra comforts Cal after his father refuses to accept the money he has made. Julie Harris was also an Actors Studio member, and her scenes with Jimmy are masterful. Both of them worked by instinct, and they played off each other to perfection. Julie Harris was later to say of Jimmy: "I liken it to a kind of star or comet that fell through the sky and everybody still talks about it. They say, 'Ah, remember the night when you saw that shooting star?'"

Right: Cal fights with his brother Aron, played by newcomer Richard Davalos. Paul Newman was originally considered for the role of Aron, but after seeing screen tests Kazan felt the chemistry between Jimmy and Davalos was more powerful.

Above: Jimmy with his script. Like other young stars, he posed for publicity shots that were designed to make his face known to the audience even before the movie was released. Although he always knew his lines, fellow actors were sometimes disarmed by the fact that he never played a scene the same way twice.

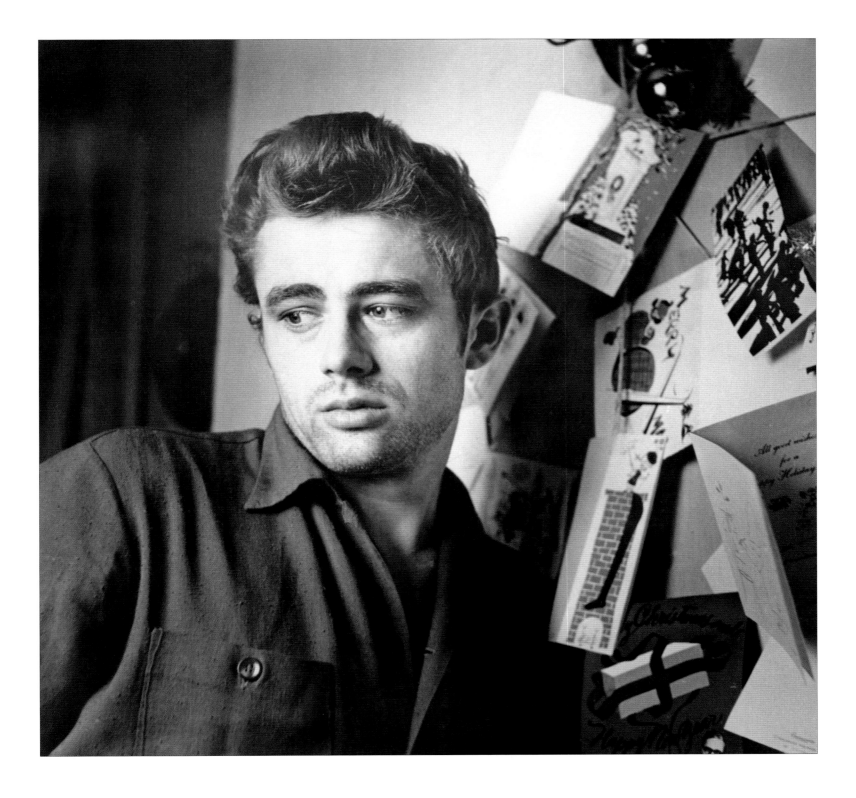

Above: As part of the publicity for *East of Eden*, Jimmy was determined to be featured in *Life* magazine. He asked his friend, photographer Roy Schatt, to send in some pictures, but although the editors liked them they wanted something more masculine. Jimmy and Schatt got together again at the end of December 1954, and for the session Jimmy did not shave or do his hair—in some of the resulting pictures he looks quite menacing. Unfortunately, they went too far, and *Life* considered the pictures too harsh to publish.

Opposite: Jimmy looks moody and thoughtful rather than wild and dangerous. At the time, movie stars were supposed to look handsome and charming—not like young hoodlums—but much of the publicity generated by the studio emphasized Jimmy's rebellious nature.

Left: After filming of *East of Eden* finished, Jimmy had some time on his hands because Warner Bros. did not yet have a new project for him. He went back to the family farm at Fairmount in February 1955 accompanied by photographer Dennis Stock, who was working on a photo essay on Jimmy for *Life* magazine. Stock took pictures of him around the town, with his family, and at his childhood haunts.

Opposite: The highlight of this trip home was Jimmy's visit to his old high school. He was invited to the Sweetheart's Ball on Valentine's Day as guest of honor, and even though *East of Eden* had not yet been released he was treated like a celebrity. The series of pictures taken by Dennis Stock was published in *Life* a few days before the premiere of *East of Eden* in New York.

Chapter Three

Rebel Without a Cause

Above: Director Nicholas Ray saw Jimmy in *East of Eden* and decided he would be perfect as Jim Stark in *Rebel Without a Cause*. The studio agreed, so the other cast members were quickly lined up: Natalie Wood as Judy, Sal Mineo as Plato, and Jim Backus as Jim Stark's father. Again, the plot mirrored Jimmy's own life to some extent—estrangement between father and son, a boy who appears arrogant but is insecure and vulnerable underneath, and a loner who resents authority.

Opposite: One of several different posters produced to advertise *Rebel Without a Cause*, which was released on November 1, 1956, shortly after Jimmy's death.

Left and opposite: Jimmy with Pier Angeli—two of the few pictures of Jimmy in formal dress. Angeli's real name was Maria Pierangeli, and she came from a devout Catholic family. Her mother strongly disapproved of Jimmy—not only was he not Italian or even Catholic, he was also surly, unkempt, and rebellious. Angeli was influenced by her mother, and so it was not surprising that she gradually stopped seeing Jimmy and finally married Vic Damone, a good Catholic boy. The marriage lasted only a few years, but by the time it ended Jimmy was dead. Later, Angeli told several of her friends that Jimmy was the only man she had ever really loved.

Right: Jimmy poses in New York before filming of *Rebel Without a Cause* begins. He had been due to start on *Giant* early in 1955, but delays in getting that project off the ground meant he had time to work on Nicholas Ray's film.

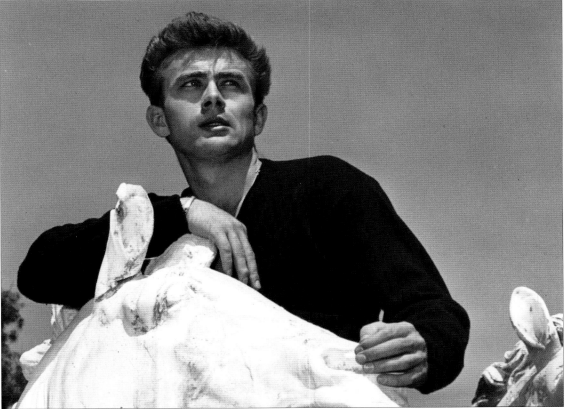

elow: Jack Simmons with Jimmy during filming of *Rebel
Without a Cause*. Simmons was a friend of Jimmy's as
well as a fellow actor, and Jimmy got him the part of
Cookie, one of the gang members.

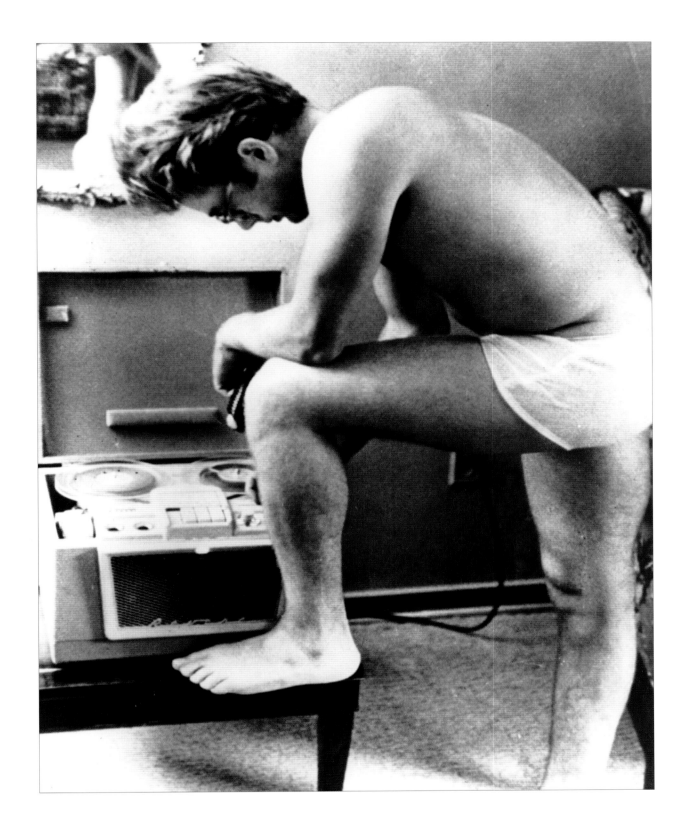

Above: Although he was not very tall, Jimmy was very well built and muscular from his years of working on the farm. He soon lost the extra weight he had put on to play Cal—at Elia Kazan's request—because it made him feel unfit and uncomfortable.

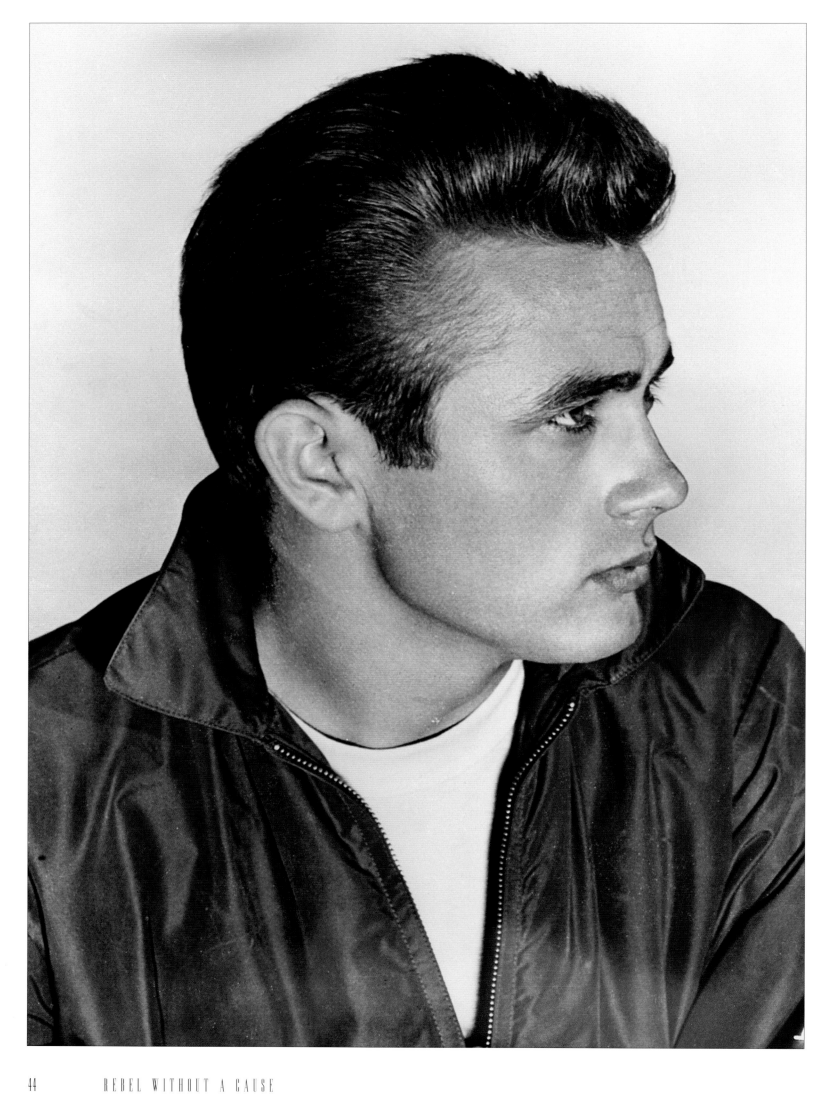

eft: Although Jimmy was twenty-three, he was totally convincing as a mixed-up seventeen-year-old student. When the movie opens he is lying drunk in the street, having gone out to escape the endless arguments at home. The following scene in the police station introduces the three main characters—Jimmy, Natalie Wood as Judy, and Sal Mineo as Plato.

pposite: After *Rebel Without a Cause* was released, the red windbreaker became a "must have" item of clothing for thousands of teenagers all round the world. The poster for the film made much of the fact that Jim Stark came from a good home—he wasn't a teenage rebel because of poverty. The story was written by director Nicholas Ray, who traveled round the country interviewing police officers and attended Los Angeles Juvenile Court to see youngsters being charged. Frank Mazzola, a former gang member, acted as consultant and also played a small role.

Opposite: Filming of *Rebel Without a Cause* began on March 28, 1955, just a few weeks after the charity premiere of *East of Eden* in New York at which Marilyn Monroe acted as a celebrity usher. Jimmy, however, incurred the anger of the studio by failing to appear at the event. His aim was to develop his craft as an actor and the glamorous life of a Hollywood star held little allure.

Above: The part of Judy was Natalie Wood's first adult role—although she had appeared with Jimmy before in a television drama called *I'm a Fool*. It was Jimmy who gave her her first screen kiss. She and Jimmy became good friends during filming, and there were even rumors that they had an affair, but Natalie was actually seeing the film's director, Nicholas Ray, at the time.

Above: Although Jim Stark comes from a respectable middle-class home, he is deeply unhappy. His mother and grandmother argue and fight constantly, and his ineffectual father—caught in the middle—is weak and self-effacing. Jimmy's depiction of pain and anger at his parents' behavior struck a chord with teenagers across America.

Above and left: Corey Allen, as gang-leader Buzz, goads Jim into a knife fight, which was very realistically choreographed. The sequence was filmed at the Griffith Park Observatory in Los Angeles, where Jimmy had made his professional debut on film in a commercial for Pepsi Cola in 1950. Jim is trying to keep out of trouble, but he cannot walk away from an accusation of cowardice, and he agrees to meet Buzz that night to compete in a "chicken run," a duel fought with stolen cars. Two drivers would race to the edge of a cliff and the first to lose his nerve and jump out was "chicken."

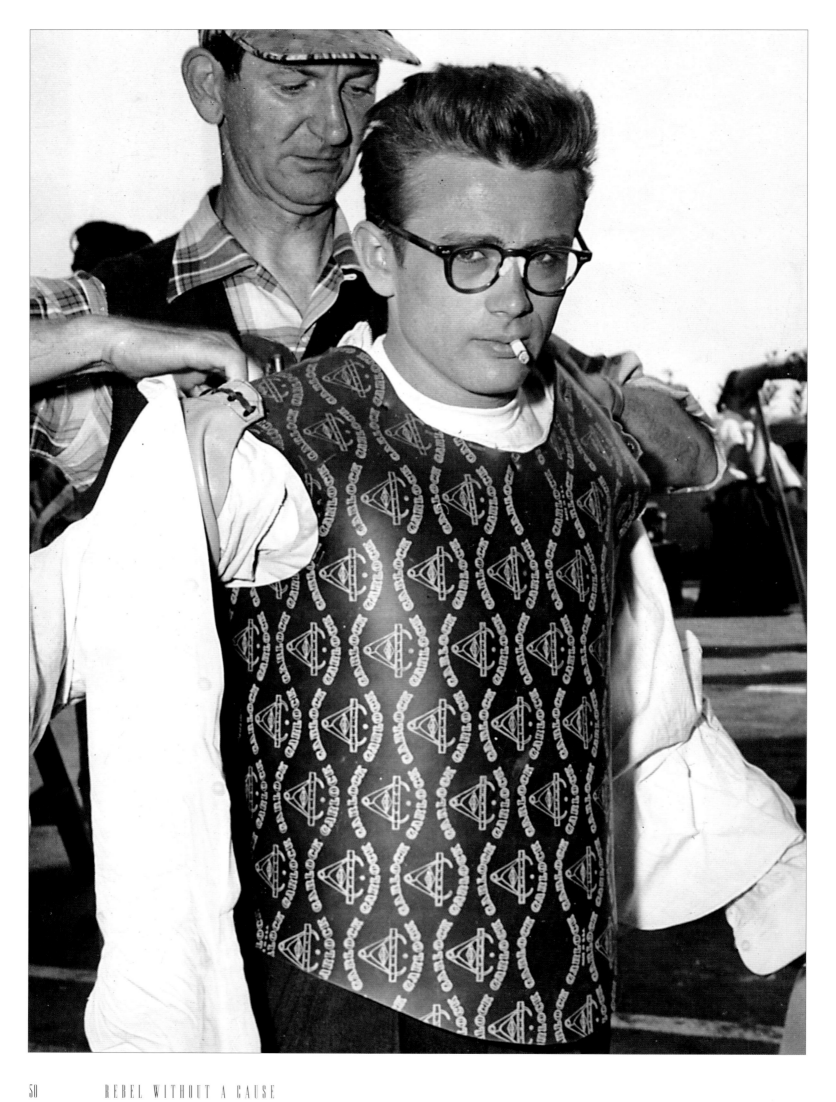

Above: Plato and Jim at the planetarium. Plato is younger than the others and he idolizes Jim. In fact, Sal Mineo was only sixteen years old when he was cast as Plato in the movie, and he looked up to Jimmy. Later Mineo acknowledged that Jimmy went out of his way to help and encourage him during their scenes together.

Opposite: Wardrobe man Henry Field helps Jimmy put his shirt over a safety vest before the knife scene. Jimmy came out of the knife scene unscathed, but did see a doctor after having punched the desk in the police station in the opening scenes of the movie. Although there were no broken bones, he was forced to have the hand bandaged.

Above: As a Method actor, Jimmy often made use of props to convey how his character was feeling. In moments of high emotion he often moved wildly and crashed into furniture, which looked very effective. However, this might have partly been explained by the fact that he did not wear his glasses for any of his film roles—and he was as blind as a bat without them.

Left: Nicholas Ray and Jimmy discuss a scene between takes. Ray allowed Jimmy so much leeway and took on so many of his suggestions that the film almost became a collaborative effort.

Below: Natalie Wood, Jimmy, and Nicholas Ray between scenes. *Rebel Without a Cause* had started filming in black and white, but four days into filming Warner Bros. decided to upgrade it from a B to an A picture after the recently released *East of Eden* began to perform unusually well at the box office. This meant that the picture could now be shot in color. Jimmy had originally planned to wear a black leather jacket, but now he picked out a red nylon windbreaker, which became the one item most associated with the movie.

Above: Jimmy between takes during the shooting of the "chicken run" sequence in *Rebel Without a Cause*. He insisted on doing the scene himself, refusing to use a stand-in stuntman, and would not allow the crew to put down mattresses to soften his landing when he jumped from the speeding car.

eft and below: After Buzz's death, the gang scatters and Jim and Judy hole up in a deserted mansion previously seen on film as Norma Desmond's house in *Sunset Boulevard*. Although Jimmy was a perfectionist about his own performance, like Sal Mineo, Natalie Wood was struck by Jimmy's willingness to help his co-stars, saying that he was inspiring, always patient, and kind. Jimmy would often stay on set to watch scenes that didn't involve him because he was interested in the whole picture and the process of movie-making.

Above: Plato comes to tell Jim and Judy that the gang is looking for them. The three of them play at being a happy family, with Jim and Judy as Plato's parents, but the fun goes terribly wrong when the gang turns up and Plato shoots one of the boys.

Right: Jimmy holds up the hand of his co-star Sal Mineo. The year after Jimmy died, Mineo made *Somebody Up There Likes Me* with Pier Angeli.

Opposite: Jimmy had a way of relating to the camera that makes many of his portraits smolder with sensuality.

Above: Jimmy is so deep in thought while playing chess that he doesn't appear to notice the bird on his shoulder. He enjoyed the experience of working on *Rebel Without a Cause* so much that he decided he wanted to do more films with Nicholas Ray. He also talked of his plans to try directing his own movie.

Above: Jim Backus played Mr. Stark, and he and Jimmy got on well. Here Jimmy is autographing a jacket for Backus, watched by Natalie Wood. In the film, in a moment of emotion, Jimmy physically dragged actor Jim Backus down the stairs and across the room—although the older man was nearly twice his weight. The violence of the scene earned the film an "X" rating in England.

Left: The classic rebel pose, cigarette between lips and eyes narrowed in concentration.

Left: Director Nicholas Ray, an unidentified man, and Jimmy pose on set. Ray said after shooting was finished that he believed Jimmy would go on to surpass most of the other stars of his generation.

Below: Jimmy clowning around on set. At one point in the filming he did an impression of Mr. Magoo, which was a private joke for those he was working with—Jim Backus, who played Jimmy's father in the picture, was also the voice for Mr. Magoo.

Above: Even before *Rebel Without a Cause* was released, Warner Bros. was sure it had a hit on its hands. Sometimes Jimmy's performance was so powerful that the cast and crew applauded on set at the end of a scene.

bove and right: Actor Tab Hunter chatting to Jimmy on the set of *Rebel Without a Cause*. Since they were of a similar age and were both handsome and talented, Hunter and Jimmy were often up against each other for the same parts—including that of Jim Stark.

Opposite: Jimmy with Ursula Andress. She had recently arrived in Hollywood, and was being groomed as a big new female star. Initially the studio publicity department had organized for them to be seen together as part of an effort to create publicity for them both, but the two of them found that they genuinely got along.

Above: Jimmy and Ursula fooling around for the camera. Jimmy told one of his friends that they fought like cats and dogs—but that making up was great fun! As well as being beautiful, Ursula was intelligent and self-confident, and Jimmy admired her independent spirit.

Above: The only thing Jimmy did not like about Ursula was her expensive taste. She came from a wealthy family and had attended an exclusive Swiss finishing school, so she was used to the finer things in life.

Left: In photographs with some of the starlets that he escorted, Jimmy often looks detached and uncomfortable, but with Ursula he was obviously involved and at ease. Their relationship broke up when she met John Derek.

Chapter Four

Giant

Above: Jimmy enjoys a joke on set. Jett Rink was supposed to be a big, beefy kind of guy, but Jimmy's performance was so riveting in *East of Eden* that director George Stevens decided to cast him despite the fact that he physically did not match the part.

Opposite: *Giant* was the picture that every actor in Hollywood wanted to work on. The book had been an immediate bestseller and Warner Bros. quickly snapped up the film rights, although it had taken some time to get the project under way. George Stevens, one of the most highly respected directors in Hollywood, was put in charge, and he assembled a star-studded cast—Rock Hudson, Elizabeth Taylor, Mercedes McCambridge, Dennis Hopper, and Carroll Baker were all well-established box-office draws, while James Dean was the studio's hot new property.

Above: A publicity shot of Jimmy as Jett Rink. Hollywood heavyweights Marlon Brando and Robert Mitchum were considered for the part before Warner Bros. settled on Dean.

Above: The so-called crucifixion still, with Elizabeth Taylor. Although one of the most famous images in the history of the movies, the scene was not actually in the film—perhaps because the kneeling Taylor seems to be subservient to Dean, which would be inconsistent with the relationship of the characters in the story.

Right: In the film Leslie is married to Texan cattle baron Bick Benedict, played by Rock Hudson. Jett Rink is a lowly ranch hand, awkward and shy but determined to move up in the world. Here he has Leslie over for tea in his shack.

Above: Jimmy, Rock Hudson, and Elizabeth Taylor during the party sequence. Director George Stevens had told Jimmy to help himself lavishly to the Benedicts' liquor, but Jimmy argued that his character should drink from his hip flask instead. He was overruled, but later Stevens said that Jimmy's idea would have been better—instantly showing that Jett was too proud to take from the Benedicts' table.

Above: Jimmy admires a model of Jett Rink's oil rig that was to be built on Jett's ranch, Little Reata. The movie was shot on location near Marfa in Texas, and although the scenes in the movie look remote and deserted, the novelty of having a film crew in the area drew thousands of local people to spectate.

Right: While he was working on *Giant*, Jimmy immersed himself in the Texan lifestyle, taking on the accent, wearing the clothes, and learning to rope a cow. His famous road safety commercial was shot during a break from filming additional material for *Giant* back at the studio after principal photography had been completed. Although he was supposed to appear as himself, Jimmy decided to wear his Jett Rink costume and performed a lasso trick with a rope.

ight: Elizabeth Taylor and
Jimmy relaxing between
takes. When they came to do
their first scene together Jimmy
was frozen with nerves, but the
two of them became firm friends
during the course of filming. They
were like brother and sister, and
she stood up for him when the
pressure of working for George
Stevens became too much.

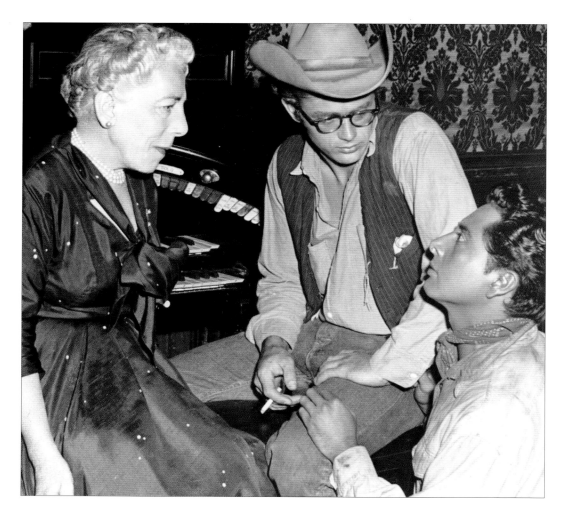

eft: Jimmy with Edna Ferber, the
writer of *Giant*. Her book was so
outstandingly successful that she
was able to hold out until she was
offered the chance to be involved in
producing the movie and a share of the
profits.

Left: During filming of *Giant*, Jimmy became friendly with Bob Hinkle, his dialogue coach. Hinkle also taught him rope tricks, and the two men would go off to hunt rabbits at night. Jimmy was often tired on set the following day—which did not amuse the director.

Above: Jimmy with Elizabeth Taylor. By the time *Giant* was released in October 1956, Jimmy had been dead for more than a year. Despite this, and the fact that his co-stars were so much more established than he was, it was Jimmy who was featured heavily in the publicity campaign for the picture. He had played major roles in only three movies, but he had been confirmed as a star as a result of the audience's reaction to *East of Eden* and *Rebel Without a Cause*.

Left: Jett may be surly and arrogant, but he is a hard worker who does not give up easily. In the book he is also savage and irresponsible, a rather unlikable brute, but Jimmy made him sympathetic, a man damaged by poverty and rejection but with an essentially good heart.

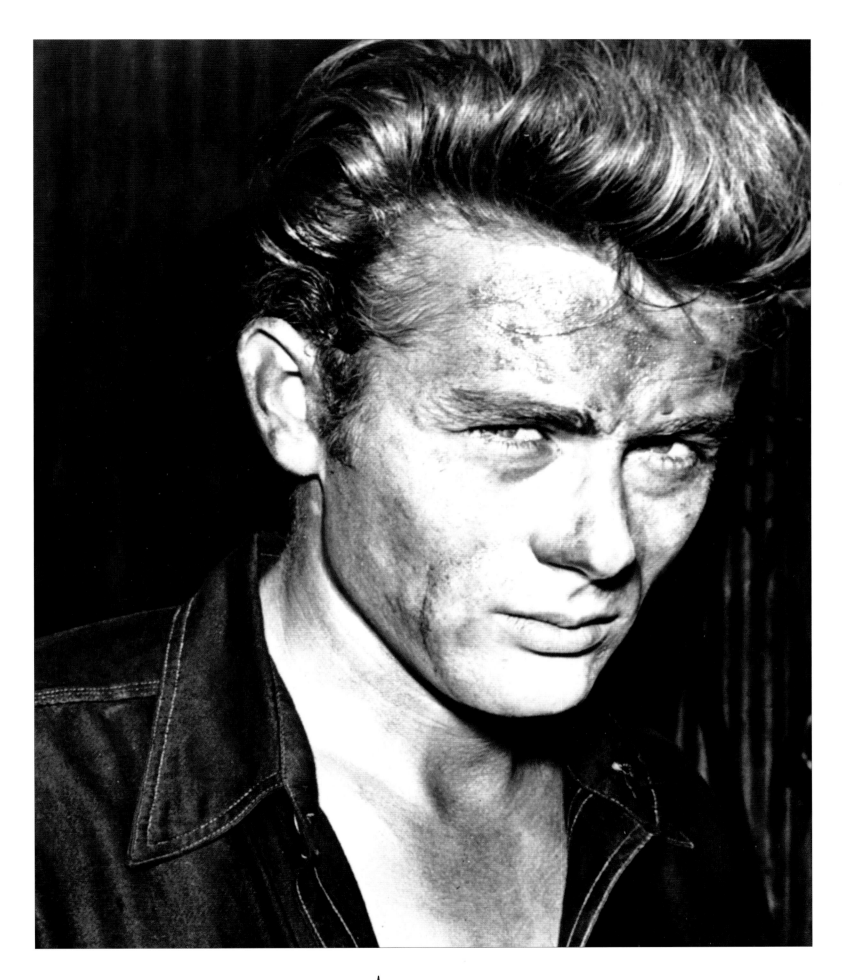

Above: Jimmy's way of working as a Method actor meant he had to get under the skin of the character. He clashed continually with Rock Hudson, who objected to his surly demeanor—and the way that Jimmy could steal a scene from right under his nose.

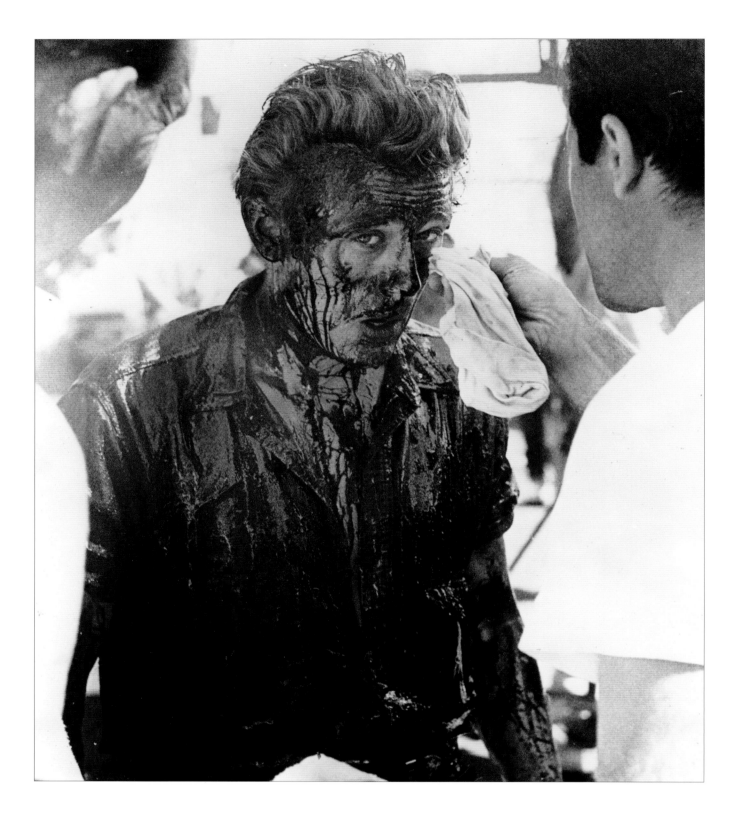

Above: Jimmy has his makeup applied for the oil strike scene. Filming was not always easy under the hot Texas sun, and director George Stevens was such a perfectionist that sessions sometimes lasted for sixteen hours at a stretch.

Opposite: Just as Jett gets down to his last penny he strikes oil on his little patch of land, and he immediately rushes over to the Benedicts' ranch to announce the news. He relishes telling Bick that now he will be richer than the Benedicts—all the years of poverty and the pent-up anger gush forth in a performance that is totally hypnotic.

Above and left: By the end of the film Jett has aged more than thirty years and has been corrupted by power and wealth. Jimmy was nominated as Best Actor for his part in *Giant*, although he was on screen for less than a quarter of the movie's length. Had he been in the category for Best Supporting Actor he would probably have won, but the members of the Academy apparently felt that his part was not large enough to warrant Best Actor, which was awarded to Yul Brynner for *The King and I*.

Opposite: Edna Ferber and Jimmy between shots during filming of the final scenes. Jimmy's portrayal of an aging and monstrous tycoon is unnerving.

Chapter Five

Genius Never Dies

Above: One of the first things Jimmy bought with his newfound income was a red MG sports car. It was not long before he discovered the joys of racing, and he started to buy increasingly powerful and faster cars.

Opposite: Jimmy was now a hot property, and his agent, Jane Deacy, was in negotiations with Warner Bros. to improve the terms of his contract. Jimmy was not only looking for more money, he wanted to establish his own production company at Warner Bros. to develop projects, and he wanted the freecom to do television and theater work. In return, he would commit to nine films for the studio over the next six years.

Above: Jimmy relaxes between races in Palm Springs, California, in March 1955, shortly before he began work on *Rebel Without a Cause*. He had bought this Porsche 356 Super Speedster earlier in the month. After winning the preliminary race for cars under 1,500cc at Palm Springs, he placed third in the finals—but Ken Miles, who came in second, was disqualified on a technicality, bumping Jimmy up to second place.

Opposite: Jimmy was a fearless driver, and professionals he raced against considered him to have the potential to become one of the greats in this field as well.

Left: Jimmy pictured with his bongo drums, which he played expertly. As he showed on the set of *Giant* when he learned to use a rope like a real cowboy, Jimmy could turn his hand to just about anything that caught his attention, and motor racing was his latest passion. However, he was also deeply interested in the possibility of directing his own movie and had carefully kept notebooks about the techniques used by the directors he had worked with.

Below: Jimmy stops to chat to motorcycle racer Ed Kretz after winning his first race at Palm Springs.

Above: Jimmy on the set of *Rebel Without a Cause* with his trophies from the Palm Springs races. There were three in all—one for winning in the preliminary race, one for second place in the main event, and the third for coming first in the Porsche class. Jimmy's first race at Palm Springs was two days before work started on *Rebel Without a Cause*. For his second race, at Minter Field in Bakersfield on May 1, 1955, he took a day off from filming. The Santa Barbara Road Races were held over Memorial Day weekend, and Jimmy managed to attend during his three days off before he joined the cast of *Giant*. While he was filming *Giant*, director George Stevens refused to allow him to race.

Above: Jimmy at the wheel of his Porsche Super Speedster. He drove this car for his first three race events, but at the final one at Santa Barbara the engine blew a piston and he had to retire it. He traded the car in partial exchange for the silver Porsche Spyder in which he died. Ironically, Jimmy shot a road safety commercial a few days before his fatal crash, which finished with him asking other drivers out there to be careful, as the life they saved might be his.

Above: Jimmy in the Porsche Spyder. The bodywork was plain aluminum, with 130—Jimmy's racing number—painted on the hood, rear deck, and both doors, and "The Little Bastard" painted in script on the tail.

Left: Photographer Sandy Roth was following Jimmy around, taking pictures for *Collier's* magazine. He accompanied Jimmy on the fateful trip to Salinas, California, on September 30, 1955, driving a Ford station wagon—seen parked behind—with stuntman Bill Hickman. This photograph was taken just before they set out.

Above: Jimmy's car, which was removed from the site of the crash at the junction of Highways 466 and 41, just west of Cholame, California. The Porsche had plowed into a Ford turning left across its path, and the impact had totally crushed the driver's side of the car. Jimmy was killed instantly, but his mechanic, Rolf Weutherich, was thrown clear.

Above: When Jimmy was buried in Park Cemetery in Fairmount, more than three thousand people arrived for the funeral—most of them friends from Indiana rather than Hollywood. Since his death, the Dean legend has been building, and thirty thousand people now regularly come for the annual memorial service that is held in Fairmount.

Left: The original tombstone on Jimmy's grave went missing twice, and it was eventually replaced with a copy that was fixed in place with super-strength glue and steel bolts.

ight: The cemetery at Fairmount is open and has a country atmosphere—perhaps it is fitting that in death Jimmy has returned to his country roots. Fairmount's connection with Jimmy has put what was a quiet country community onto the international stage. People travel from all over the world to attend the town's annual Museum Days, which are held alongside the memorial service and feature a variety of events—some connected only loosely with Jimmy himself.

eft: The year after Jimmy died, Steve Allen devoted an entire show to him, and several family members appeared. Seated, left to right: Mrs. Charles Nolan Dean (Jimmy's aunt) and Emma and Charles Dean (grandparents). Standing, left to right: Joe and Betsy Dean (cousins), Charles Nolan Dean (uncle), David Dean (cousin), and Steve Allen.

bove: James Dean fan Carol Brousseau, pictured with her collection of memorabilia. In the years after Jimmy's death, so many companies tried to capitalize on the Dean name that the Winslows hired a management company to license its use. The family objected to some of the objects on offer, and these were soon removed from the market. Sales of posters, postcards, T-shirts, sunglasses, replica red windbreakers—and hundreds of other items—now generate millions of dollars of income every year, which is split between the close family members.

Above: Jimmy as he is remembered by many in the role of the teenage rebel who seemed to speak for his generation. *Rebel Without a Cause* started out as a low-budget B movie and has become an enduring classic of the cinema.

Opposite: Jimmy and Julie Harris in an intimate moment from *East of Eden*. Part of Jimmy's appeal was that he could show great tenderness as well as convincingly play anger and frustration.

Epilogue

James Byron Dean died on September 30, 1955, at the age of twenty-four. Despite the fact that only one of his movies had so far been released, the national newspapers quickly picked up on news of his death. Although Warner Bros. was devastated to lose such a talented actor with such great potential, the studio was surprised at the sheer number of obituaries in major newspapers and magazines. However, studio executives expected that after a short period of mourning the name of James Dean would slip back into relative obscurity and never could have imagined he would become the legend he is today.

When *Rebel Without a Cause* was released in November 1955, the story, coupled with Jimmy's tragic death, caught the imagination, and touched the hearts of those watching the movie—here was an image of doomed youth, lighting up the sky with an intensity of emotion, and then gone forever. Rather than just a promising new star, Jimmy was rapidly becoming an icon for a generation. When *Giant* was released the following year, everyone wanted to see Jimmy in his final role, completed just weeks before he died. His performance was stunning, and his reputation grew even greater.

Since Jimmy's death, the Dean myth has grown steadily stronger, year by year. His is one of the few faces that is recognized just as easily and quickly in almost every country in the world as it is in America, and some thirty thousand fans descend on his hometown of Fairmount, Indiana, every year for the memorial service on the anniversary of his death. Jimmy may be dead, but the James Dean legend will live forever.

Chronology

1931

Feb 8 James Byron Dean is born in Marion, Indiana, to Mildred and Winton Dean

1936

Summer The Dean family moves to Santa Monica, California

1940

Jul 14 Mildred Dean dies of cancer

Jul Jimmy is sent to Fairmount, Indiana, to live with Marcus and Ortense Winslow, his father's brother-in-law and sister

1949

Apr 8 In the first round of the National Forensic League state speaking tournament, Jimmy wins with a performance of "The Madman's Manuscript" from *The Pickwick Papers* and goes on to become state winner

Apr 29 Jimmy is placed sixth in the national tournament

Jun 15 After signing up for pre-law classes at Santa Monica City College, Jimmy leaves Indiana to live with his father in California

Summer Jimmy joins the Miller Playhouse Theater Guild in Los Angeles

1950

Fall Jimmy transfers to the University of California at Los Angeles, because it has one of the country's best theater departments, and moves onto campus

Oct During rehearsals for the UCLA performance of *Macbeth*, Jimmy meets Bill Bast

Nov Highly regarded agent Isabelle Draesemer comes to see *Macbeth* and signs up James Dean as a client

Dec 13 Jimmy gets his first paid work as an actor when he appears in a Pepsi television commercial

1951

Jan Bill Bast and Jimmy move into an apartment in Santa Monica

Feb Jimmy gets the part of John the Baptist in a television movie, Father Peyton's TV Theater *Hill Number One*, which stars Roddy McDowall and was to be aired that Easter

Spring Jimmy meets Beverly Wills, and they start dating. He drops out of UCLA

Summer After a series of disagreements with Bill, Jimmy moves to the Gower Plaza hotel in Hollywood

Summer Jimmy meets advertising agency director Rogers Brackett and soon moves into his apartment on Sunset Plaza Drive, off Sunset Strip. Rogers gets him work on a series of radio shows and bit parts in films

Oct Rogers Brackett leaves for Chicago to work, and Jimmy goes with him

Oct Jimmy briefly visits his family in Fairmount

Oct Arriving in New York, Jimmy first stays at the Iroquois on West 44th Street, but soon moves to the West Side YMCA

Nov Jimmy gets a job pre-testing stunts and warming up the audience on the game show *Beat the Clock*

Winter Jane Deacy, then at the Louis Shurr Agency, becomes James Dean's agent

Winter Jimmy meets Elizabeth (Dizzy) Sheridan, and they become close friends

1952

Mar Rogers Brackett comes to New York, and Jimmy soon moves into his apartment on West 38th Street

May Bill Bast comes to New York after graduating from UCLA, and he and Jimmy take a room together at the Iroquois

Summer Christine White meets Jimmy in the office of his agent. She is preparing a scene to audition for the famous Actors Studio and invites him to perform with her. They are both accepted

Summer Jimmy takes Bill and Dizzy Sheridan to stay with his family in Fairmount

Oct Jimmy is offered his first big part, in a play called *See the Jaguar*

Dec 3 *See the Jaguar* opens on Broadway, but closes on December 6 after devastating reviews—although the critics speak favorably of Jimmy

1953

Feb 8 Jimmy co-stars as Bob Ford, the man who killed Jesse James, in an episode of *You Are There* called "The Capture of Jesse James"

Fall Jimmy is offered the part of Bachir in *The Immoralist*

Dec 18 Rehearsals start for *The Immoralist* in New York

Christmas Jimmy visits his family in Fairmount

1954

Jan 9 Tryouts for *The Immoralist* begin in Philadelphia

Feb 1 Previews of *The Immoralist* begin in New York

Feb 8 Opening night of *The Immoralist* on Broadway, with Jimmy turning in a stunning performance and getting rave reviews. Jimmy leaves the production almost immediately, having been offered a leading role in the movie *East of Eden*

Mar 8 Elia Kazan, the director of *East of Eden*, and Jimmy leave New York, heading for Hollywood

May Jimmy buys a red 1953 MG

May 27 Filming starts on *East of Eden*

Summer Jimmy starts dating Pier Angeli, a beautiful up-and-coming actress, and they become a hot item in the gossip columns

Aug 9 Filming wraps on *East of Eden*

Aug Jimmy returns to New York for two weeks

Oct Pier tells Jimmy she has decided to marry singer Vic Damone

Winter Jimmy returns to New York

1955

Jan Warner Bros. calls Jimmy back to Los Angeles to decide on his next picture

Feb Jimmy takes photographer Dennis Stock to visit his family in Fairmount during the course of a photo essay for *Life* magazine

Feb Jimmy and Dennis go to New York to continue the photo essay

Mar 7 The photo essay appears in *Life*

Mar 9 Premiere of *East of Eden* at the Astor Theater in New York City. The celebrity ushers include Marilyn Monroe and Marlene Dietrich, but Jimmy does not attend

Mar Jimmy buys a 1955 Ford station wagon and a 356 1,500cc Porsche Super Speedster convertible

Mar 26 Driving the Porsche, Jimmy wins the preliminary race at the Palm Springs Road Races in California and is placed second in the finals

Mar 28 Filming starts on *Rebel Without a Cause*

Apr Jimmy starts dating up-and-coming star Ursula Andress

May 1 Taking a day off from filming, Jimmy races at Minter Field in Bakersfield, where he is placed third

May 23 Filming starts on *Giant*—but without Jimmy, who is finishing *Rebel Without a Cause*

May 26 Filming wraps on *Rebel Without a Cause*

May 28 Jimmy drives in the Santa Barbara Road Races over Memorial Day weekend

Jun 3 Jimmy joins the production of *Giant* in Texas

Jul 10 Most of the cast and crew of *Giant* leave Texas, but Jimmy stays behind with the second unit to complete his solo scenes

Jul 12 Jimmy leaves Texas to rejoin the rest of the company in Los Angeles

Sep 12 Main filming on *Giant* wraps

Sep 17 Jimmy is filmed for a television public-service commercial on safe driving for the National Safety Council

Sep 21 Jimmy trades in his 356 Speedster for a new Porsche Spyder 550/1,500 RS

Sep 30 Jimmy Dean is killed when his Porsche plows into a Ford turning left across its path just west of Cholame, California

Oct 8 The funeral is held at Fairmount Friends Church, and Jimmy is buried in Park Cemetery

Oct 11 The coroner's inquest concludes the crash was an accident, and that the other driver, Donald Turnupseed, is not to blame

Nov 1 General release of *Rebel Without a Cause*

Nov 25 *Collier's* magazine runs a photographic essay on James Dean

1956

Summer The James Dean Foundation is incorporated in Fairmount to raise money to support young actors trying to break into show business

Oct 7 Two thousand people attend a remembrance service held at Park Cemetery in Fairmount

Oct 10 Premiere of *Giant* in New York City

Oct 17 Premiere of *Giant* in Los Angeles

1957

Fall Release of *The James Dean Story*, a documentary made by Warner Bros.

1970

Sep Warner Bros. re-releases *Giant* and fans wait in line to see it

1974

The Eagles record "James Dean" for their first album, *On the Border*

1975

Fall Fans organize memorial services in several U.S. cities

1980

Sep Thousands of fans turn up for a memorial service in Fairmount

1983

Mar Warner Bros. re-releases *Giant* and fans stand in line round the block to see it

Apr 12 The tombstone on James Dean's grave is stolen, but is found on May 6 at a crossroads a few miles away

Summer The tombstone goes missing again

1985

May A replacement tombstone is put on the grave, fixed in place with steel rods and super glue

Sept Warner Bros. re-releases *Rebel Without a Cause* and *East of Eden* and fans again wait in line to see them

Sep Los Angeles declares September 30 to be James Dean Day.

Fairmount now calls their annual event Museum Days/Remembering James Dean and plans for fifteen thousand people to arrive

1987

May 24 The original tombstone from James Dean's grave is found in Fort Wayne, Indiana

1992

Sept Thirty thousand people attend Fairmount's Museum Day

Filmography

PLAYS

1952   *Woman of Trachis*

      The Metamorphosis

      See the Jaguar

1953   *The Scarecrow*

1954   *The Immoralist*

FILMS

1951   *Fixed Bayonets*

1952   *Sailor Beware*

      Has Anybody Seen My Gal?

1954   *East of Eden*

1955   *Rebel Without a Cause*

1956   *Giant*

TELEVISION

1951   *Father Peyton's TV Theater* "Hill Number One"

      The Alan Young Show

      The Web

1952   *Tales of Tomorrow*

      Studio One "Ten Thousand Horses Singing"

      Kraft Television Theater "Prologue to Glory"

      Studio One episode about Abraham Lincoln

      Hallmark Hall of Fame "Forgotten Children"

1953   *You Are There* "The Capture of Jesse James"

      Kate Smith Hour "Hound of Heaven"

Treasury Men in Action "The Case of the Watchful Dog"

Danger "No Room"

Treasury Men in Action "The Case of the Sawed-Off Shotgun"

Tales of Tomorrow "The Evil Within"

Campbell Sound Stage "Something for an Empty Briefcase"

Studio One Summer Theater "Sentence of Death"

Danger "Death Is My Neighbor"

The Big Story

Omnibus "Glory in the Flower"

Kraft Television Theater "Keep Our Honor Bright"

Campbell Sound Stage "Life Sentence"

Kraft Television Theater "A Long Time till Dawn"

Armstrong Circle Theater "The Bells of Cockaigne"

Robert Montgomery Presents "Harvest"

1954   *Philco Playhouse* "Run Like a Thief"

      Danger "Padlocks"

      General Electric Theater "I'm a Fool"

      General Electric Theater "The Dark, Dark Hour"

1955   *U.S. Steel Hour* "The Thief"

      Lever Brothers' Lux Video Theater "The Life of Emile Zola"

      Schlitz Playhouse "The Unlighted Road"

AWARDS

1953-4   Daniel Blum Award for Most Promising Stage Personality

      Antoinette Perry Award ("Tony") for Best Supporting Actor on Broadway

1954   Theater World Award as Most Promising Newcomer for *The Immoralist*

1955   Filmdom's Famous Fives Award

      Hollywood Foreign Press Association posthumous Golden Globe Award

      French magazine *Cinémonde* Best Foreign Actor for 1955

      Modern Screen Special Achievement Silver Cup Award for 1955

1956   *Photoplay* Gold Medal Award posthumously for Outstanding Dramatic Appearances

      Academy Award nomination as Best Actor for *East of Eden*

      New York Film Critics Circle nomination as Best Actor for *East of Eden*

      French Film Academy Best Foreign Actor for *East of Eden*

      French Film Academy The Crystal Star

1957   Academy Award nomination as Best Actor for *Giant*

      French Film Academy "Winged Victory" for Best Actor for *Giant*

      Hollywood Foreign Press Association World's Favorite Actor

Index

A

Academy Award nominations, 9, 78
acting, first interest in, 15, 16
acting style, 10, 17, 32, 33, 52, 61, 75
actors, relationships with, 9, 11, 31, 33, 42, 55, 62, 72, 75
Actors Studio, 19, 25, 32
agents, 19, 81
Allen, Corey, 49
Allen, Steve, 90
Andress, Ursula, 62–5
Angeli, Pier, 31, 40–1, 56

B

"Bachir," 21, 22
Backus, Jim, 39, 59, 60
Baker, Carroll, 67
Battle Cry, 20
bit parts, 23
bongo drums, 84
Brando, Marlon, 68
Brousseau, Carol (fan), 91
Brynner, Yul, 78

C

"Cal," 11, 25, 26, 32
car racing, 17, 82–5
camera, relating to, 10, 16, 56–7
Carey, Timothy, 27
cars, 81, 82–8
chicken run, 49, 54
childhood, 13–18
Collier's magazine, 87
contracts, 81
crash, 88
"crucifixtion" still, 69

D

Damone, Vic, 41
Davalos, Richard, 29, 31, 32
Deacy, Jane, 81
Dean, family group, 90
Dean, Mildred (mother), 13, 15
Dean, Winton (father), 13, 25
death, 88
DeWeerd, James (Rev.), 17
directing plans, 58, 84
directors
    Kazan, Elia, 25, 27, 30
    Ray, Nicholas, 39, 45, 47, 53, 58, 60
    relationships with, 27, 58
    Stevens, George, 67, 70, 76
Draesemer, Isabelle, 19

E

East of Eden, 10, 21, 53
    cast, 31
    filming, 27, 29–31
    publicity, 24, 34–5
eyesight, 18, 52

F

Fairmount, Indiana, 13, 15, 36
    High School, 18
    memorial service, 89, 93
    Museum Days, 90
    Park Cemetery, 89–90
family, 13, 15, 16, 25, 90, 91
fans, 91, 93
farm life, 17
father, 13, 25
Ferber, Edna, 72, 78–9
Field, Henry, 50–1
Fixed Bayonets, 23
funeral, 89

G

Giant, 9, 41
    book author, 72, 78–9
    cast, 67
    filming, 70–7
    publicity, 66, 68, 74
    release, 93
Gilmore, Jonathan, 22
glasses, 18, 52
Gordon, Harold, 31
Griffin Park Observatory, 49

H

Harris, Julie, 31, 32
Has Anybody Seen My Gal?, 23
Hickman, Bill, 87
high school, 18
Hinkle, Bob, 73
Hopper, Dennis, 67
Hopper, Hedda, 28
Hudson, Rock, 67, 69, 70, 75
Hunter, Tab, 20, 62

I

iconic status, 11, 89, 93
I'm a Fool, 47
image, 10, 11, 35, 59, 93
The Immoralist, 10, 21, 22
Indiana, 13, 17
Ives, Burl, 29

J

"Jett Rink," 8, 9, 67, 68, 70, 71, 74, 76–8
"Jim Stark," 45, 46, 47, 51
Jourdan, Louis, 22

K

Kazan, Elia, 25, 27, 30, 43
The King and I, 78
knife fight scene, 49–50
Kretz, Ed, 84

L

Life magazine, 35, 36

M

Macbeth, 19
McCambridge, Mercedes, 67
Marion, Indiana, 13
Markie (Marcus Winslow, Jr.), 16
Mazzola, Frank, 45
memorabilia, 91
memorial service, 89, 93
method acting, 10, 19, 32, 52, 75
MG sports car, 81
Mineo, Sal, 39, 51, 56
Minter Field races, 85
Mitchum, Robert, 68
mother, 13, 15
Mr. Magoo, 60
music, 29, 84

N

New York, 19, 22, 23, 41
Newman, Paul, 32

O

Osborn, Paul, 25
Oscar nominations, 9, 78

P

Page, Geraldine, 21
Palm Springs road races, 81, 84, 85
Park Cemetery, 89–90
personal relationships, 31, 41, 62–5, 73
Pierangeli, Maria, see *Angeli, Pier.*
plays, 10, 20, 21, 22
Porsche 356 Super Speedster, 82, 86
Porsche Spyder, 86–8

press, 28
publicity, 28, 33, 35–7, 62, 68

R

Ray, Nicholas, 39, 45, 47, 53, 58, 60
rebel image, 10, 11, 35, 59, 93
Rebel Without a Cause
    cast, 39
    chicken run sequence, 49, 54
    filming, 42–3, 50–4, 60
    knife fight, 49–50
    publicity, 38, 45
    release, 93
relationships
    with directors, 27, 58
    with other actors, 9, 11, 31, 33, 42, 55, 62, 72, 75
    personal, 31, 41, 62–5, 73
road safety commercial, 71, 86
Roth, Sandy, 87

S

Sailor Beware, 23
Santa Barbara road races, 85, 86
Santa Monica, California, 15
Schatt, Roy, 35
Scissors Dance, 22
See the Jaguar, 20
Simmons, Jack, 42
Smith, Lois, 30, 31
Stevens, George, 67, 70, 76, 85
Stock, Dennis, 36
style, 40–1, 44, 53, 65

T

Taylor, Elizabeth, 67, 69, 70, 72, 74
television parts, 20, 47
theater, 10, 20, 21, 22
tombstone, 89

U

University of California Los Angeles (UCLA), 19

W

Warner Bros., 36, 53, 61, 67, 81, 93
Weutherich, Rolf, 88
windbreaker, red, 44–5, 53
Winslow, Joseph, 13
Winslow, Marcus Junior (Markie), 16
Winslow, Marcus (uncle), 13, 15
Winslow, Ortense (aunt), 15, 16
Wood, Natalie, 9, 39, 45, 47, 53, 55, 56, 59